CHRISTOPHER GASKINS
Boys have been...

SIBLING RIVALRY PRESS
ALEXANDER, ARKANSAS
WWW.SIBLINGRIVALRYPRESS.COM

Boys have been . . .

Copyright © 2013 by Christopher Gaskins

Cover art by Chris Thompson

Author photograph courtesy of Christopher Gaskins

Cover design by Mona Z. Kraculdy

All rights reserved. No part of this book may be reproduced or republished without written consent from the publisher, except by reviewers who may quote brief excerpts in connection with a review in a newspaper, magazine, or electronic publication; nor may any part of this book be reproduced, stored in a retrieval system, or transmitted in any form, or by any means be recorded without written consent of the publisher.

Sibling Rivalry Press, LLC
13913 Magnolia Glen Drive
Alexander, AR 72002

info@siblingrivalrypress.com

www.siblingrivalrypress.com

ISBN: 978-1-937420-51-2

Library of Congress Control Number: 2013945840

First Sibling Rivalry Press Edition, October 2013

FOR
KELLIE SCHLUSSEL,
BEST FRIEND EXTRAORDINAIRE

Boys

Stephen's Body	11
he was	12
Another's Regards	13
Dancing Alone with Darren	14
Sexed	16
Violet	18
for Louis	20
K.C.'s Persistence	26
One Night Stand	28
Demons	29
Exorcism	31
To get to my heart	33
Love and Life	34
for Jason	36
Returning Home Enamored at 4 A.M.	43
Drew,	44
Exeunt	46
Boys Have Been	47
for Paul	48
Bedtime Story	53
The Floor, Again	54
for David	56
The Men at The Metro	62

have been ...

Days Like This	63
for Hiram	65
The Beautiful Freak	70
First Date	72
Afternoon Lover	73
for James	74
Ulterior Motives	80
All of My Amorous Rage	82
4th Night with Patrick	85
That Solution	88
a blowjob	90
When you left, Mike,	91
Too Cruel Anywhere	93
for Shawn	96
The Last Time I Loved Him	99
cold	102
hot ass	104
Names, Like Fingers	105
Here	107
Sunday night out in the East Village	109
for Steve	111
How Obvious, Then	121
Acknowledgments	123
About the Poet	124
About the Publisher	125

Boys have been...

Stephen's Body

At twenty-two
I fell in love, but not without a
naïve grace,
though shredded in the end like an obscene thought,
dumped out of mind
like some water-logged rock, an
overlooked obstinacy.

Still, supposing it all
in that invisible stretch in-between
your lips,
in the edible fatness your eyes averted. I only
found our moment
after it was over, unfurnished, un-
hidden. Not unforgettable—

the effortless sighs,
a tortured vowel in search of sound or
some semblance of life
slithering around the mouth,
whimpering, wanting.
Your arms made it hard, a loud enough crawl
of your fingers

through the dark, getting closer to me and
my open-palm waiting.
I coerced the blame, gave into my panic and vague
intuition.
I fondled the surface, damnation deflating
with a reluctant hiss, a wrinkling
of purpose.

HE WAS

        he was something
    special,
            voodoo swimming in heaven

Another's Regards

The shame that comes,
originating
underneath your words, from around
your tongue, is the one

he implied when he sang
"hellooooo,"
when the echo his shoes made
ascending the stairs

dug into the silence, my
smile
of assurance. The chill as then
shivers here in winter,

in this mechanical warmth, stale red
and slow-
burning browns. Like blades
and scabs, I know of Hell—

he laughed to flick between thumb and
finger
a trail of winks and giggles. I
followed his meaning

just hours ago on the club's
verandah
as we left together. Yet, how can I fight your
sleep, your snoring?

Dancing Alone with Darren

There is no
body, only flesh
for miles
unseen by eyes and

gripped,
a grudge with a dagger's
plunge, an
eightball eye roll

and flaccid feint.
Beguiled
in turn with the bile to bear
bizarre ingrown

burns, each pelting-rain
kiss
like this to hit your
asphalt angles,

smooth, smoldering shoulders,
groped
for lust and a surge
like hair.

Daring discordance or a
liquid-eyed look,
confusion in
pupils now widening, livid

around the quick, pin-
prick of effort,
wetter
than depth, waiting longer to linger,

fall
closer to this: the snap
of air
between us broken.

Sexed

Two halves collide,
connect.
I'm filling up faster, beyond all meaning. Yet, I
linger on empty,
aware of that something more wicked
than waiting
at the foot of the stairs.

Just follow my fear
down the steps of my spine, then out of each crevice
like fire
melting butter. Our slip and slide
fetish,
a kiss full-lip tickle of unshaven gravel
as I curl at the edges,
go thick
and I harden,
a rippling outward of pliable tension. He divides
my hesitation into equal cut pieces, into
leg silhouettes
at right angle shapes, a weightless
egress.
        In him,
evil slavers with pleasure,
it has hands
with rake-teeth fingers to upturn every sin
buried deep in my skin
and warmth in his palms and wrists and
knuckles.

Former gods unveil. I am
closer to breath, exhaling Pompeii. Final curtains
have parted. The
defiler
has entered, now glistening
red as he slithers in deeper, along
perimeters
           and into the
Garden.

Violet

The
fist as a phallus
barreling over itself only to emerge
again, entwine
headfirst

from
out of the unlit hemorrhaging maw
of your anger's
heart, in arc and drop at angled
descent,

fingers
bent-double in making their
stand. I am our
bull's-eye whirlpooling down, all aglow,
come

hither
against my own subconscious, still
yearning you forward
in turn, with each toss of my
beckoning

damage
and plaster-lipped smile, the
bloom, implosion
of masochist's love. The air-
split

arrival,
your hardened intent
hurtling into
and out of my expression's unknown
depths.

For Louis

1. *Afternoons with Louis*

Why is it I need you

like helium balloons, like
fingers holding up
the corners of a smile? Awaiting in
patience
the stories you promise

to finish up later, leading me further and closer
to a pot-of-gold pleasure, an
afterglow of anticipation.
Why is it so
that I have to have this, our wind-

thin embrace every time
we hug,
every time you blurt, "And how
have you been?"
The afternoons I sat and festered, calmly

sipping water because, as you said,
it was all you had. I give
them back—that
gist I held while on my way over, the
song "Possession," Mrs. Parker's poem, your

worries heaved in all directions,
a picture painted
in shades of gray; though, come tomorrow, needing still

to have and hold
the phone whose bridge will never burn.

    2. Error

I've turned into
for you, for you, the walking waste
flung far away

yet coming back with fingers
tapping along
your shoulder, halfway meeting

the bend then fold
of a crimson colored, dried-up
papier-mâché

expression. I am quietly
waiting, although
this is not

exactly what you've said to do
or asked of me.
You turn your head.

The men entwine with every step,
alone, among,
you're never there, not one

of them,
the reared and ready, well-dressed you who
guards the bridge

that's never crossed
and only littered by yourself.
Still, I

would slide like shaken water,
take my stand
to rise as smoke that's

crawling open at its center
outward, seize
what no one sees, gather up, all over

handle what you've hidden
inside the drawers—
worn-out lusts like old cadavers.

    3. Louis at 3 a.m.

What does it mean to dream that I'm dying
with the syrupy, lip-
licking thrill of an orgasm?
To plummet, to
drown,
to writhe in angina, see-saw in fever,
have nightmares of Louis?

I dream of you talking
and showing me doors, taking us
on tours of
strange, underground houses where you won't
hold my hand,
only cologne-hot mirages left
floating in bedrooms.

I'm burning to breathe
the musk of your armpits,
slither my face
in among the copper-red hair that softens

your chest
and waist, your innermost
thigh,

to perch your punitive hallway of flavors
on the tip of my tongue
like a word
or answers I'm trying to remember. It
fades then dwindles.
I lick my lips
but nothing remains.

    4. Amputation

It is gone and I've been cheated
out of the rush
of cooler air, the whir and
swoosh

that would, of course, have marked
its passing.
I stagger off-center,
rubbing where it should have been, this limb

of love I'd nicknamed "Louis"
and used
to handle everything. I'm not unlike
a newborn leper,

learning over every trick and
way of doing,
still sprawled in fits of compensation, mute and
mouthing

misquoted outbursts, floating upwards
through dementia,
pale and pink.
There's nothing quite like it

though it throbs in haunting, carves me off
from inspiration,
all the movements I've half-
forgotten.

5. *Excuses for a poem*

Sorry, you, you're
out of luck. They don't exist, though

still you argue, "Yes, they do.
I've seen them, heard

them hiding before." I cannot
hold my head up higher,

lick my lips
or bear it longer, crave

the rush
which stills the ripple, moves

to place it as it wasn't.
As I sit here,

there you go
to scrape the sink's cold rusted bottom with

bell-shaped glasses
sloshing over; gulped, eaten-up

placebo handfuls,
smiles that stay and keep us calmer,

stand in place when
lyrics murmur,

poems prick and
what is said is finally said.

K.C.'s Persistence

You are
as you were—red-faced, with a deeper
odor
of sweatier curves and
something else, something purring in every
pore of your
sunburned skin, oily

and freckled, something aware of only
itself with each of its
hindered, hovering movements. You're leaning in
forward to rub
my shoulders and remove
my shirt,
increase your efforts,

slur
the words that would barely stop this,
the heat of you
wearing just your shorts, now
squeezing us closer.
I dread each tickle of curly
brown hair

that sprouts in waves from throat to waist
and disappears.
It makes me cringe, to sit imagining
where it goes, this
sudden attempt,
your urge
which throbs staccato

throughout your fingertips.
Kisses nicked
on the back of my neck go unacknowledged, chances
lying in untold
inches
I know you wish would
come together.

One Night Stand

I left off lying
when last I spoke, smiling at us like an air-
stuffed,
pink and shiny, balloon-faced
fool, trembling
then giggling, dribbling a language
in lines of drool
wiped away
with four casual fingertips. You
are staring.

Tell me what
I am whispering now, then—truths which
spew
like curdled milk or
something else that's in a hurry
unto itself
in half-born phrases? Our
bigger breaths
and we are through with touching. We
are bored, sprawled
in throes of acquiescence, naked skin
against the carpet,
all at once
behind the curtains, talking
nonsense.

Lies emerge from each abyss of
untapped hurt,
that tattered wear of re-used looks, out over the
ledge
of moving lips and we
are drowning.

Demons

Daddy, we never talked
about Marjuan—
your coworker, friend, our neighbor or whatever
he was
to you; to me
he was the man who took
my clothes
off when I was eight years old.

Even now, daddy,
your wrinkled-up, snickering face, the
days
when you drank and cared
about nothing
still block my periphery. I can't
bring to mind
what Marjuan really looked like or any expressions

he might have worn
if I'd have scratched his surface.
I only see
in shades of tan his full-
length cock, I
only feel
his two dirtied hands pushing me eagerly
towards it,

I only smell
the salt of sweat and glistening
precum,
a tangle of pubic hair

catching my tears.
When against my will and thinking of you,
your reluctant fathering,
I believe you both

were not much different.
I only taste
the dick-flavored vomit still burning
its way upward, I
only hear
the names you called me when I finally
left.
But I try to forget.

Exorcism

Bitter it isn't, this
rock-bottom rage, out of nowhere anger neither born
nor bred, just
plopped down inside me, kept
slithering in

place for month after month, dispersing
like worms and leaving
the scene of
origin only to poison the limbs, then
curdle the conscience.

I love you like this where I sever bare-handed
air we had breathed,
your attention which scurried for
a blond-haired
replacement. It took no time at all.

My thrown-up lunch
was as yet still warm in puddles rippling atop
the carpet.
Every light bulb here, now, is either
loosened

or gone. I'm in a dark more blue
than black and passing this Marlboro phallus from
fingers to
lips, lit red in the glow
of its cremating tip,

curled on the couch with my feet
underneath me, inhaling
smoother,
ignoring the creeping-in, cancerous effect, the
slackening body.

It all runs over—
the squishing and squirming of
festering hatred.
I've yet to forget your sudden amnesia as I
stood there in quicksand,

waving and nodding as if I were
stupid
and somehow confused. Politely, I smiled, said "hi"
to your beau
in the sweetest of drones, bearing my burden:

a remembrance of you
fully mounted behind me and gasping
"I love you"
as your emptying penis convulsed in erection,
burrowing onward

and past the hipbone, held in place as I alone
rose up to melt,
split not
unlike a passage home, two
halves divided.

To get to my heart

you must split my ribs and
rub them brittle,
snap my spine in several places, grab
and grind
then shove aside the
sweeter excess,
dig for love with a higher fervor like digging
a hole
to China and back;
the dirt never seems to fit in exactly
the way it came out.

Love and Life

Love and life
and all therein, including lust,
have left me cold
against
the bathroom's linoleum floor, curled upon

its convex patterns, faded
patches
gray in color with slip-resistant
topography.
I have seen it all

up-close and rested
hands
across its surface many times in prolonged
moments,
touched myself

then thought, "Why bother?"
Groped to hold
my will together, failed, gone
limp,
balled the dust between two fingers,

let it drop. This floor
can't feel my slow caresses, lies there
chilled
and growing tepid,
breathes

horizons along my body.
I endure
the empty roar of an unfed stomach, other
voices,
boys who never hung around

in fettered whispers.
The unswept floor implies a patience
devoid of words.
Both our reflections
cease to ripple.

Life dead-ends and hits
the baseboard.
Every urge to rise and stretch recedes,
gives way
to stoic floating.

FOR JASON

1. Inquest

Surely, you like me? You did,
once,
at least "at first" in a
prologue someone

forgot to write. Your name and number,
a handshake, even,
and then a game of telephone tag
dwindling out . . .

You're it. You're it. You're it. It's your
turn now
and I won't wait. Instead, I walk
throughout my house,

touching objects, setting them right,
moving them
only to put them back, ignoring
the ring

the phone doesn't make. Oh! and
there's nothing on TV,
no dinner to cook or reason to fold the sheets
and quilts,

to sweep the floor. Sunday
has come,
the weekend's over and I can't bear
to ask anymore,

fondling then fumbling
the hem
of my shirt, the button on my shorts.
So much, I guess,

for crucial chances, that one-on-
one whoring
I never got around to actually
doing.

    2. Mistaking Jason's Directions

I am standing alone,
loitering
in among my improvised poems cautiously whispered
over and over, eyes
half-closed. Another peek confirms,
confuses.

I tilt my weight
from foot to foot to
leaning against
a wall, a window, a rhythm inherent in running,
unraveling
back to my car. Suddenly,
somewhere, I know

that something has stopped and stood and
dug in its feet,
drowning in steam and pivoting forward, finds
disappointment
like water
where sand becomes mud. At the end of your directions

and still empty-handed,
apathy
strangled by anger and sadness. My heart
tipped crooked
in every option withering breathless, left to listen.
I'm done with knocking
or trying again.

Prurience licks its catalyst's wounds. Then
I wander through
an adjacent building, find
another number 102. The door swings open. You lie
on the verge
of an indirect greeting.

3. In an Aftermath of Boys and Boys

It comes again
like airwaves on acid and I
am screaming,

clawing away at calm assumptions,
manners minded
and everything after.

Lips deserted,
habits
hanging around as always: me alone

with someone's absence. The
bell below
forgot to toll and toppled over. Fist

by fist
in facial image knuckle-deep,
now non-cohesive,

incoherent.
Nothing breeds a barren something.
Plaster cracks.

One day I'll ask
how you
could still be smiling as

"you and I"
abort inchoate, wilt away. Or
did you kick it,

nudge its nose when I wasn't looking?
Either way
you smirk as though

I cannot see it, roll your eyes
and hope I'll leave.
Yes,

you fooled me.
You win the medal.
Give me quick

a sharper edge on which to
straddle,
to balance recovery.

    4. Stubbed My Big Toe

Stubbed my big toe and
didn't know
that I wasn't worth it. Falling in favor,
like weather, with you
comes and goes.

We've ways of getting around our anger,
shoving it firmly

under the skin, inhaling
our hatred.
When I dare to think, I believe
you're a bastard:
your cap on backwards, wearing circular-framed
schoolboy glasses,
grinning

with only half of your mouth. My
days are identical,
whether watching Bugs Bunny
or reading Dostoevsky—
an atrophy
of sadness rivets my heart then renders it
useless,

ricochets inward. I lie on the carpet,
sit in an armchair,
run to the phone when there isn't
a ringing.
On long afternoons with the windows wide open
all that lingers
is a faint aroma of rotting raindrops,

of something coming.
It isn't me
through your endeavors, hands
or lips.
This freeze of rage
is self-embalming, like Tori's music; out of sync
with soothing boredom.

5. Jason and His Kind

I suppose, then, it goes
like this—
I'll sit at home without the right
to youth's insouciance,
twiddle

my thumbs and breed my ulcers,
tangle my hair.
You make me sick though still excite me,
leave me
with only hallucinations:

your lips, your hair-covered chest,
callous hands
and a hardening penis
laid out before me like candy on quicksand,
thirst

then drowning.
Inside each clump of miniature time
that slim
black
snooze button on my alarm clock

gives me, the dreams
it sends me
scurrying back to with eyes half-closed and
in those dreams,
Jason,

his kind,
are fucking and fucking me. My

showers are hot,
my blankets are clean.
On any night

I wait and wait and wait and
wait.
My telephone number
has never been changed but it just might
as well be.

Returning home enamored at 4 a.m.

is unexpected.
You were Eunice's friend and that
was all.
As I usually do,
I took you in from head to toe, you and
all

of your drunken friends, you
and all
of the other boys
around the room, inhaled the mood
at once
and coughed and knew

I wasn't perfect.
The way you grinned and laughed too loudly,
embraced
the bartender, appeared so friendly,
a reflection
of lights in your

perspiration.
We shook our hands
when she first introduced us. I smiled,
but you
were looking elsewhere, sauntering on. Yet,
it doesn't matter—

last night we kissed and danced together.

Drew,

tonight I love my god in your direction,
unfold my heart
like a stored-away lawn chair and
defer all dying.

Any chance at all through sought-after coincidence
implies, of course, inherent
confusion,
the piranha nibbles of every cliché: you, how your love
is "too good to be true." I reject, I
entice.
I struggled like Lazarus
for three cold days following our
initial flirtation, when
you finally emailed, "Hey, man, what's going on?"
I scowled,
        but answered,
rewording my fate with dubious hands. I
swallowed the hook.
                Since then,
we've talked on the phone,
spent nights together.
Like a scratched-up record you repeatedly claim, "I won't let you
let me go"
with epic intentions, a grip on our future like
old world myths and
Zodiac arrows, a resentment of science
as sterile and stagnant.

When you speak,
                you tell me

of heartbeats and honor, the collision and melding of two
        broken
halves.
I listen, my head is against your chest. There is
already mention
of "husband and husband," oaths
and a core of amelioration—you, the savior
of our incurable sadness.

I tingle with instinct, fathom your image
in collective pieces, yet
                  you laugh
as I tell you
how I only believe in superheroes, in promises able
to leap tall buildings and
outrun
        distance.

Exeunt

You licked the lips
of every boy,
began at length with all their moans

held

like breath
or leaking mouthfuls of indiscretion.
Swallowing

hollow. You,
in one
great ball-and-chain blink,
threw away
your subterfuges and left me as only
lovers will do,
pranced and swayed
and reeled them in, both tongue and tonsil—
nothing less
than the heart's pied piper

and nothing more.

Boys Have Been

London Bridge keeps falling down, these
boys have been
my root of evil, sticking

things
in hard to reach places, along
each crevice. So,

yes, I let all those handsome creeps and losers
spread my legs
and fill me up with spurts

of acid, scalding streams of pure-
white nothing,
forget to thank me. I would, for once,

like to hold a hand
instead of a hard-on, all lathered in love
without a residue.

None of them know
while they're ramming it into me any thoughts
I think,

the books I've read or the poems I write.
A fuck is a fuck
as my heart collapses.

for Paul

1. Dear Paul,

This slew of words, this poem, is the "first of many."
It's our little joke.
With imprints of pink and unseen bruises
distorting my ears
from
hours and hours

spent talking to you
with the telephone pressed
to the side of my head, I'm lost and losing
piece by piece
the gist of time, yet gaining momentum.
Lying on the carpet,
my fingers wade into and out of my hair from scalp

to tip, listening to you speak,
a sweet
murmuring voice that incites arousal,
an articulation of resonant
warmth.
My lips are moving

in sync and licked to a velvety wetness,
kissing against
the smooth hard plastic
where your words ease through like an embrace of
insights.
Everything aches in silence
after you've finished. The hunger

lengthens;
loneliness stares up at my ceiling with eyes
like spotlights, fearing
a life
that is merely parasitic, tired of giving up as well as giving.
But now there's you

and hope in handfuls, unlabored
effort, as
out of a mind like mine always breeding possibilities
ripe for slaughter,
one question comes and anything else
comes down to this:
would you and I embrace and dance,

slow and close,
our arms and bodies supporting our weight,
hands that slide from
neck to waist,
kisses crawling from shoulder
to lips?

My thoughts and nudity dwell and shiver
as daylight approaches.
I've dreamt
without sleep, no routine of movement from bed to
bedroom, here to gone.
A flock of hallucinations lift,
are weightless.

    2. I Just Want to Be Perfect

This second poem
is of an ease much easier than breathing, but
swallowing air can lead

to choking,
fear itself, the fear of failure,
of being a fool when you walk through my door
on your very first visit
and I hug you,
squeeze you into a sudden reality,
believe for once that
now
I have everything.

(This embarrassing lust for you,
as a whole,
is eroding my patience.)

3. So, I Stole That Book (On Our First Date)

I've done it again. What's done
is done.
The issue not being, as you lecture me, whether I'm
"fragile" or not
or whether I'm inconsiderate.
You shake your head
and through clenched teeth breathe a
fogbank of anger.
You leave me voiceless as though I've been slapped

with the utmost care by your
disbelief
in the gentlest rage that's almost afraid
of its own velocity,
stumbling around, in a head-on
frustration
against rolled-up windows.
You're driving me home after an Italian dinner,

after Barnes and Noble,
the book

I stole
now lying in the floorboard next to my shoes. You suggest
that maybe I did this to poison
my image
and push you away. (Come on, give me a break.)
"Is this something you do a lot?"
Well,
what if it is?

    4. Second Thoughts

All right, Paul.
Never before have I ripped up a poem,
rubbed out words
with a loser's frenzy, a calloused

palm, or scratched away at nice
neat lines
with chewed-down fingernails. (However,
they still don't care,

those unknown secrets, batting their eyelashes
in omens of failure.)
If you peek in on me this afternoon
you'll see

a tempest of limbs intent on slaughter, a
decimation of language.
Clawing, severing
with a carnivore's shame, locating the itch, my own

hopes murdered, skinned and eaten
by me—the bulimic.
(Poor baby, this victim: a helpless ream of
unlined paper.)

Not quite. It's a shattered
funhouse mirror. In shards and shreds
I still look ridiculous,
with my eyebrows furrowed

in embarrassed confusion.
You left me last night, swore you "couldn't sleep."
It was four a.m.
and today these poems no longer matter.

Bedtime Story

These are things
that stick like glycerin: you, your

fingers,
a sweat-slick quilt
as we float
beneath it, heathen in creamy

anonymous dampness.
Our hair
clings together like saltwater taffy. All
limbs and crevices
slither entangled, smolder
then glisten.
               And, yet,
my love,
there is blood in our breathing.

The Floor, Again

Today it has gone with the clanging
of chains, the ripples and
wrinkles of a selfless core, you
falling from your fingertips. There
is the floor

and my resistance upon it, a
shapeliness wrought
out of form-fitted shards, left-over
atrocities. You're dancing
in echoes with a mouthful of grins, a face

I've hated for too many moments
and domino minutes, empty
marathon grips. Wrapped now in old
touches, still
suspicious of every

repetition and lisp, mangled
aftertastes lingering
and not letting go. No affection to pummel
this five-
fingered self, my lust

for regrets,
phallic butter-soft thoughts. Forbearing
arousal, acquiescent diversions. You
never do fade
with your abrasive expressions, your

perennial mumblings
and yells to behold a tattered
elasticity dangling
like Rapunzel's own hair,
again dirtied and dirtied with only

promises, promises.

FOR DAVID

1. November

The heart, perhaps,
was made
to swelter in thinning absence, to
float in place,

that something borrowed, something blue.
We gag on love
as colder hands scoop down
around it—

ten thin lines of ten below zero.
Voids grow rotten.
The season has shed its selfless rhythm,
its sadness like thunder.

2. A Nice Quiet Neighborhood

Echoing belches
of odor beneath every rock upturned, all this
airborne anger,
          the spit of fits
polka dotting
the winds like mismatched sand
shaken clean from a living room rug.
We hate our boredom,

filling the house
with secondhand smoke, bills unpaid and recurrent
migraines.

                We only embrace
to make a point,
unless today is a day that can make us sick
(and there are many of those).

This morning, the mosquito-bite
nitpick of voices
at 7 a.m.
from a next door yard sale and we are interrupted,
walking around
as we wake up slowly,
mumbling,
"So, what are we going to do today?"

      3. distant and cold

"It's no wonder," you say,
"that my friends and also my mother have found you to be
distant and cold." Even
    here,
your words are too warm for comfort.

      4. I Almost Cheated on You

Colder linoleum
with winter outside, a withering
freeze
and here, the side of
the bathtub
offers me a way to get back on my feet. But not

today.
The pure taste of vomiting is a warmth
that escapes, like

metallic rain and arms uplifted
in a long
cold shower. My heart

sliding liquid then out through my bowels and
into the light
blue toilet. The red mosaic
dissolving
and trembling, chipping in slivers. I can't get clean.
I am only empty, yet

overflowing.

    5. I dislike

least of all this: one syllable
sounds,
equivocal anger,
some tap water leak from your fountain of words as I

wallow in puddles.

    6. Dear David,

It has come to this and as it comes, this
is how I see it:

our six-month love affair
was only
a break between the violence with
Robert (your ex-)
and now.
Three years declined in short-sighted habit. After Robert
I was there to find you.
We moved your belongings like midday burglars.

I bought you clothes
to replace the ones you said Robert had worn
and ruined while painting,
CDs he'd scratched
came back new to you as Christmas gifts.
When you yelled at me

I always took it
and put it away where I understood.
Can second chances
make up the difference, a void like
hate?
Now suddenly you tell me you'll always love him.
Will you love him each time
he's erect
without protection? Sex
soothes a heart too tired to break.

Days fill up
with all your things still
here, still
warm—these photos
of your grandparents which I framed myself
as a birthday present
that still sit poised on the kitchen
counter. I clean
around them. They smile at me. We are
awkward
here to be waiting for you.

      7. *Eeny-Meeny-Miney-Moe*

I caught a boyfriend
by the toe
and that regret has left me whole

like plush
stuffed animals filled with snow.

My hands are cold.
We lie together
beyond our prime, on into habit. A comfort worse
than nothing better.
We grope and slip and slowly strangle.

    8. *David Came Home*

David came home
while I was taking a nap.
His father called and
they laughed
about David's new start with his ex-boyfriend Robert,
laughed
about visiting
there sometime during Easter.

David came home
to sleep as a vacation from sleeping
with Robert,
as a breather from friends still
sharing a joint.
I heard him singing while doing his laundry,
swelling with pride and plans
for the weekend,

for having someone to hold.
I held
my hands and arms together under the pillow,
curled my body

and cried
but the couch, its cushions, could not
console me, not with
David at home.

The telephone rings.
It's for David again. I sit up slowly, my hair
sticking out
and call his name to say "hello."
He doesn't hear me,
laughs
then whispers.
I'm crying for you, for us, for Easter.

The Men at *The Metro*

Along the edge of fornication, I
stagger,
absorb the hint of nearer misses. Every man
at once self-conscious,
elbow-deep,
embracing his efforts. Men in handfuls,
cluttered, shirtless, shifting

men
and me among them—gods to any unvarying degree in
our theme song blankets
lowered upon us,
sweatier sounds we interpret differently
as flickering lights

replace the heavens; hardwood floors and walls
of mirrors, of carpets
strewn like hair below the navel.
Men belong here,
boiling within their own debris of eyes and
grins,
accidental erections.

Days Like This

6:35 a.m.
in a living room that has no furniture,
I sit on the carpet, my legs
in a "V"
with a collection of socks—I can't find a pair.
(They're all the same color.)
The walls are empty.
I'm not going to work and I don't have a reason, only,
"It's freezing and windless."

On days like this one,
at 7 a.m.,
where a grayish-blue world
bottoms-out,
or might, to an afternoon heat wave, humidity swells,
puffing up like leeches
in secondhand sweat. My back is turning.
I still haven't dressed.

And Cameron has told me, "I really
respect you," but
he has a boyfriend already and said, "I just can't do this to you."
And Jason? Oh!
I almost forgot about him. He never did call.
It's days like this
that I'm there again on our hotel balcony
with Brian beside me
in Orlando.
We're talking and lean on the railing, our arms outstretched.
It's warm and windy.
"I want to jump, you know," I said. "There's nothing

to stop me." He's almost crying.
Yet, I don't remember
if Brian suddenly embraced me or moved any closer, when
he whispered, "I'd never recover."

Brian isn't my boyfriend or lover and never has been,
but on days like this one,
leaning
to peek out from between the curtains, alone, I know
his friendship has ruined me.
At 5 p.m.
nothing else happens.
Through these locked, sliding glass doors
dusk breeds momentum. There's
no one to love.
I've left my imprint: two hands, an expression.

It's colder than I'd expected and
the leaves are shaking.

for Hiram

> *1. Unrequited*

I have seen you,
distinct among all distractions, your profile, expression, you
in passing,

a glance at you
from around each corner, you with your secretive
cinnamon places.

I stand erect
outside my classroom door and I watch you walk, inhale
each scent

of your body
cascading around you. You, like hypnosis, are an act of believing.
Would a smile undo

all those weeks of longing and me: the image
of something
beyond your notice, a something

crushed
with that sudden heel of a shoe, an accidental embrace.
I'm returning to you

like mud
in the warm brown sky of your eyes. I fly
then float. I save.

I remember. We were glowing like Sodom, I dreamt
late on a school night,
entwining in fire, we two boys together,

caressed by thunder, Edgar Allen Poe kisses—our heights
were wuthering.
Yet by day we continue as

teacher and student,
a familiar plight beguiling us forward, that keeps
composure.

2. Your Insight Isn't

Your insight isn't what I want it to be.
For you, articulation
is half the problem. You choose your words as you
would choose
the least painful method of dying.

Like too much rope, I hang
on every sentence
we do not need. You should only say
what you always mean
when you write your poems. Do away with clues;

these hints in a crevice are a casual match, a
fire of cancer
in my interpretations. You dare
to ask me,
"So, what do you think of this poem?"

Our secrets refracted,
we avoid abstaining and speak
to listen,
though a poet's heart is born with bruises, the ice
too thin for mutual truces.

3. "The Intellectual Lover" - a reply

I "comprehend" your "message." It is not a message
but rather
an SOS from your own subconscious.
Every thought is symbolic.
In the glances you scatter with half-closed eyes

pure truth is discerned. Fear
mutilates vision.
I am before you, in reach. I am an icon of trust.
We discuss philosophy. We are
speaking to one another in poetic delusions.

4. Feel, Then Know

The mood that moves you
is subtle
like gray. Your intentions ablaze
as fingernails
scrape the back of your scalp
from the inside-out.

Poetry tickles
then twists its blade.

You "hold your thoughts" in a highbrow place,
but drops of words
collect in sewers, drown aesthetics.
Every day
you burn like summer, sweat
covers my body—

a tidal wave slap
of black and blue morals.

5. Pronouns in Poetry

It's always either a "she" or "her." I can
no longer take it.
Why am I not where I should be?
Standing here in disbelief,
you, like God, are everything, a love
created in my own reflection
but you won't admit it,
hide the "he" in peripheries. Your
words deny.
As always, I keep reading in-between your lines.

6. Love is not this

Love is not this:

that graceful stride of intent
you have
in approaching me and then walking right past.

I am clumps of air.

In the unborn language of your teenage heart
my name is unsaid.
You are walking to class

and I am old, left

standing here merely in a breeze like
winter, blind
in the glare of your insensitive nature, a

silhouette against clouds.

7. Well, Hiram,

I suppose it's pointless to think of you at all
like this.
You are not
of "Christopher and his kind."
Even so,

the poetry between us was almost love.

The Beautiful Freak

In the car with Heather
at eleven o'clock last Saturday evening
and nervous,
I reclined my head like an ugly duckling against the seat,
curled and stretched my legs, rubbing them
together.
For an hour, with the windows partly rolled down,
rabid autumn breezes
throttled
and slammed each cigarette
back and forth between my lips and long white fingers.
Our small talk deepened.

You were waiting inside a downtown
gothic nightclub,
surrounded by friends adorned in mourning. We sped to you,
that club our climax, this blind date's
backdrop.
I'd already heard so much about you—"a beautiful freak."
Yet, you raped my breathing, you
in the midst
of an LSD nightmare and rhythm for demons happily
dancing in Hell.
You sat perched in your chair
and shook my hand,
                held it—

I skydived and hovered in air tainted orange, bluish-purple
and red,
every painting that hung on impressionist walls
I hit
like pinball,

came returning to you, soft through the crowd like
astral projection.
                        You,
laughing and yelling and almost obnoxious,
your teeth glowing fluorescent,
a worm-crawling warmth of sounds in my ear and suddenly
we're whispering—
our words slip together as
leftover pieces.
Your arm is around me.
You burn in my periphery, a rumba of frightening
paper doll cutouts:
your head completely shaven except those
four black spikes
on top with pink-edged tips,
nose ring
and tongue ring, four earrings at once,
elastic black shirt
and black vinyl pants, enormous black knee-high boots,
a green dragon tattoo
on a smooth, sparsely-haired stomach,
a spider on your calf,
silver rings and half-hidden necklaces, . . . And me?
I watch

as your eyebrow arches, innuendo
groaning
behind every sentence, a sneer at once both subtle and twisting
itself, its subtext,
into smiles of purpose, the lips of an abyss,

the night just beginning . . .

First Date

Watch his face
as he sits
together with one knee up and one knee
down—perpendicular comfort,
casual placement.

He's talking low and his legs are
naked
against the sofa. A cotton
softness surrounds
his body: large white t-shirt, shorts and boxers,

athletic socks (his shoes
are off).
He props his arms
into awkward places, by his side, in between
himself

and his shih tzu dog, scratching
in leisure
what's really not itching, even
caressing his hair
finger by finger and leaning his head.

He watches your face. He hears
you speak,
is trying to touch you without ever moving,
scattering smiles.
You kick off your shoes.

Afternoon Lover

You start your horrors like
engines,
caviar or cadavers, events of the heart

capsizing us all. We prolong our
moments, recline
at bedtime luxuriantly victimized—a film star

who's fallen, still waiting
for you, for
all that you offer like tip-toes in toffee,

verandahs, horizons, a spotlight
in daydreams.
You rip with vehemence right into existence

the sum of your absence. You
leave us unbridled.
We search with our hands and plunder the secret: me,

myself, my infallible image. We've loved you
like whores.
We've eaten with whispers the salt

of your fortune, now tonguing out shrapnel
still lodged
in the teeth like remnants of ardor.

FOR JAMES

1. James,

this morning I stopped
and thought
of you as if under hypnosis,

ran a hand
along my body, a hand that you
had somehow borrowed

through my own subconscious.
I bit my lips,
held back a smile too big for wearing.

2. A Poem on Saturday

I stayed in bed until 11:37
and almost missed "X-Men." It was a rerun anyway.
In disappointment
I went back to bed, turned on the fan,

but Saffie, my tan and white shih tzu puppy,
rolled over
and gave me kisses. We went for a walk
and I knew that you

would want to know that today
is a day still undecided—
shiny and warm and perfectly placid,
then shadowed as

clouds growing gray in the middle
buried the sun
in their gyrating folds and leached out its light;
the air smelled damp,

all leaves and branches shuddered in warning
and again it was sunny.
I sat on the porch and graded some papers.
At 1:53

I drove with Saffie to Popeye's for lunch,
listening to Enya,
Sade, your voice in memory.
The windows were down

and the day didn't know
yet if there is going to be rain.
At 2:46 I am home
and anxious, now writing this poem. Outside

there's thunder.

    3. *Ballad of Boredom*

I forget the name of that cologne you wear.
I don't remember
things or details and didn't think
about you needing a ride to the airport on Monday
after your upcoming visit.
(How naive, how awkward it progresses,
these internet begun,
long-distance relationships.) On the telephone, sometimes,
I'm way too silly
and talk too much. I sing off-key,

mention lyrics to songs
that I want to send you and you laugh "oh, no."
I fear
every song dedication must be
a ballad of boredom,
stupidity,
or a crime of redundancy. I make mistakes
in raising my worth,
read aloud Spider-Woman comics
(even changing the voices)
when you're not in the mood; it must be awful.
My affection for you
creates an imperfect image; in that way
I am perfect.

Now, you are no longer writing me poems.
I'm waiting for you
to break my heart in a loss of interest, spit in the face
of all that I stand for,
leave my hopes,
as low as you found them.

    4. Morning

You learned the language
much too easily,
now speak like a native, your very first visit, here in this black
and blue backyard jungle of a deaf-mute
heart
at once overfilled
with blurs as communication and
unmade sounds.
                  My home, not unlike
a Garden of Eden
strangling in weeds and ill-kept

words;
all answers lie in root,
      in ore, underneath your footfalls.
You are standing,
creeping within to a place
like this
where I'm waiting to hear any secrets you speak
in affection's
own impurity of language.

  5. *Afternoon*

To love you, as if loving you were something
even halfway conscious
or lesser than this:
     the clump and clutter of a thump-
numbing heart,
the rise
of you in LSD visions and Technicolor hue,
the asthma grip of that
sidelong space in the big wide bed
you will not relinquish
for another night.
     For now, we swim in a handmade scent
of sweatier parts,
the roar
of anything assumed, explainable.

  6. *Evening*

The bedroom is dark.
We sit
  apart like breath and breathing, linked across
an unseen limbo
of conversation like clouds and air, as

black as depth.
                  We reach. We stretch. We are
as one
and distance melts.

       7. "the one" who wasn't

Many poems, (well, ones like this one),
pertain
to "the one" who certainly wasn't, the one who wrote and
mailed me poems,

sang sweet little promises
out of tune,
who believed half the time that
my name was "baby."

       8. Sudden Discomfort

Two weeks of planning stop
short,
are over. You've canceled your visit. Only this

remains: a gangrenous

goal, every earlier hope now limp and
soggy
like carry-out leftovers, used-up grayish-blue
sparklers, fireworks

that could've been white-hot rainbows.

You should know what it's done,
what hurts, what
hits.

From two hours distance you can hear
my heart shred

like cheap polyester.

Ulterior Motives

John buys me things. There are no hidden reasons.
He is adamant about this, he
hugs,
        caresses,
slithers out words of reassurance, beholds me
fatherly, fondles
the hair around my elbow.
"It's love
within friendship," he rehearses in earnest on a spur of the
moment. Even then
his fingers
circumscribe calmly their provocative circles
across my shoulder
over
and over, him leaning in closer.

John buys me breakfast, lunch and dinner. "Well,
it's only practical. You have to eat."
He pays my phone bill,
drops in to visit
while I'm busy at work and slips me
money
inside of a small white envelope. "For gas. I know
I don't have to."

(John imagines in secret and acts
accordingly.)

We meet on Sundays and I read him my poems

like vicarious foreplay. He'll
cry,
     then laugh,
even rub my neck to relieve all tension,
touch
my body in platonic massages. "You know, without the shirt
it'd feel a whole lot better."

I dream as seeing,
imagine our lives enacted—both bull's-eye, periphery—
in the seat of
          your lap, John,
with you as some white-haired jolly Saint Nick or
beckoning grandfather
only wanting affection in full-bodied
theory,
a kiss and his due in smiling impatience. I fidget, then wake and
I wonder

why you're being so nice.

All of My Amorous Rage

I'm not that ugly, but to you
I'm expendable. I correct my posture, try
on smiles like
beacons
of varying sizes. Nothing helps.

You throw me away so sweetly, so gently,
it's hard to be angry.
I am only one man in a medley of these, as loved or
lonely
as he or him and hardly
worth mention.
Even so, you acted on third or fourth thought,
created,
        demolished
our mirage of history. We're lost in nowhere. Your insouciance
is evil
in a sip untasted of so much beauty, a god-
like aura. Why, last weekend
as I was leaving with Heather, did you touch my shoulder,
ask me
        "What was your name again?"
after several months
when, like an unwanted gift, I had given it to you.
Even then, you were gentle, nodded
in smiles,
politely held on until it was over.

All those weekends following, you changed your expressions,
whispered with friends,
danced

calmly and cool,
forgot that you'd met me.
I wallowed in haste, set aside all sadness—
last night it rose,
it slapped my heart in a sharp resurgence, broke up my being,
brought me over to you
to say "hello," make conversation, then hear
you say,
        "I'll talk to you later," touch me and leave.

There is only this inside my embarrassment: your two topmost
buttons undone, your
chest of hair
to which my libido had just born witness, slow
thick rolling sweat
sliding in unheard places,
charcoal resentment
                and rage
like a turn-on.

So I left you alone,
stood soothed in shadows, benign with confusion,
aware
as you moved
like a thunderstorm with a center of stillness
through lights, as you leaned
from bar stool
to stranger, your stance a prediction
to which I referred all stratagems. This—my longing,

an amorous phallus that shivers and shifts
enclosed in its silence,
a study in kinetics, heating
in ripples
throughout its adamant spinal-length core to echo,

foreshadow the
zeal

    of a bullet.

4th Night with Patrick

Lust defrost in an overdue
blood flow,
warmer, for once, on our first night

alone.

All words dissolving, how we turned ourselves on. A trembling
inferno,
a conflagration, sizzling pavement
beneath the sun,
razors and race cars, a rabid
infection,
a pulsating Adonis in
red iridescence.

You were burning my body from the outside in.
I could taste
your last cigarette, our kiss
gliding sour,
encircling our tongues. Our heads and groins like hot lava
pistols.
We ate without temperance, outlining
our mouths, our chins
and necks
in gilded saliva,
felt the needle-point pin
prick
of facial hair stubble scratch across our lips as we
lapped up sweat with carnivorous

thirst

in the furnace of your idling car.
We nibbled and
bit
and slid our hands in
below the belt line, contorting our crotches,
grinding
our cocks up into the air
with the shivering
thunder
of techno rhythms throbbing the stereo speakers, ripping
off clothes
in a parking lot space far away from all lampposts.
We sucked. You

swallowed.

I clawed at the seat cushions, tore at my
hair,
snagging my composure on hooks of euphoria, slurring
moans of acceptance,
merging
      "Oh, fuck!"
and
    "Oh, God!"

into realms of new meaning. I craved your essence. I wanted to
taste it
like simultaneous
withdrawal and addiction, the
culmination
of all of your body: sweet liquor of semen, those velvet-
soft hairs
threading your stomach,
your beautiful hands intertwining with
mine,

brown eyes without end,
your smile that

incited

these heart-attack orgasms, this frenzy of being, my mouth
on your erection,
your nipples, your hairline.
For over an hour
we writhed in our flames, our delicious
hungers
and so help me,

I loved it.

That Solution

Even though I threw up love
like a stomach
full of aspirin, you held on,

    oblivious,

to the back of my head
half-buried beneath the cool cotton of two fluffy pillows, still
murmured "poor thing"
as if you were expecting magic, a hotter
exhaling
of sweet-nothing intentions.

I relinquished the evening, the dinner,
the movie.
I hated you then,
like needles jabbing into every pore of my skin,
my forehead bruised
with burrowing worms and tight little veins
of serrated
        lightning.

You tried to kiss me.
Inside the blackout, this migraine lobotomy, curled-up
in quilts,
to feel your tongue and lips

    emerge

against my own with no preclusion, hint
or warning

is unforgivable. Your breath was stale, your mouth tasting too much
like an old chicken sandwich.

You left and came back, leaned onto
the bed,
       whispered,
"Is your headache gone yet?" then kissed me
again.

A BLOWJOB

About blowjobs, let's see. . . .
Does it lead to love
if you loiter your hands all over his body,
rise
to kiss him and again descend,
if you lick each nipple,
his shoulder, his stomach? (Well, maybe it doesn't.)
In ordinary daylight,
at least,
I've discovered that a blowjob in theory
can take away boredom,
watching
a crotch that appears to breathe with its curves
and creases,
an ebb and flow in men who approach or
stand
or sit. There's a tickle, a hiss
beneath every expression
I layer, when smiles
fall
half-off their hinges, when men disappear and potential erupts,
the eyes
move elsewhere.

When You Left, Mike,

which was worse,
that my intentions leaned over and I wanted to kiss you
or that I failed to do it?
Standing too long, but not long enough
beside your car in the 2 a.m.
cold,
we witnessed our postures starving for warmth
with mirrored
         shiverings
inside of their thin layered pre-winter clothes. I fought
the urge
like a slow tug of war. My fists
which burrowed, shook down up-against the seam-corner
bottoms
of each coat pocket
and then emerged—two impulsive limbs
caught coming together,
crossing the chasm
grown fatter
         between us.
I embraced your jacket like crinkling blue skin, desiring
to slither my half-warmed fingers
around your ears
and whisper confections, the liquor of truth
like an Indian summer, how
badly
      I'd dreamed

for the last two hours, stretched
side by side
in bed, watching that documentary but seeing instead
the blankets divide us,

all valleys and hills down the legs of your jeans, both hands
enfolded and
lying
across your stomach—those straight
black hairs
along the back of each wrist
severed
by the red plaid cuffs of your long-sleeve shirt,
your Italian profile
reflecting
the colors of TV images; unshaven cheeks,
a droop of the eyelids, the tongue
at times
that would lick its lips. I was afraid to indulge, slide
elbow
        then arm
any closer together, trip us up
downhill
in a caress by accident. We spoke about nothing.

At 1:58,
that awkward habit of shoes then jackets being put back on, a
glance
at the door, an escort following you step by step
and out to the parking lot.
You needed again
my telephone number, unsure of how, exactly, the first one got lost.
We grinned
too many new grins for profit. You
told me
how you hated the weather,
unlocked your car door loudly, deliberately, confirmed
my directions back to I-95,
got in
and were gone.

Too Cruel Anywhere

It is the first mistake, my leaving like this, taking
all three bags too tightly zipped
and filled
with thrift store shirts, baggy jeans and
black vinyl pants, the shorts and t-shirts I never did wear,
my platform shoes, my sandals, socks and boxers,
books and even
some Christmas presents, taking more
than I'd brought
back
through state after state to an empty home
in snow
and leaving you, alone and warm in southwest Florida,
five months to wait until I return
the way
I left. By then
what else will you have felt?

Sitting here now on this airplane, I run
out of running
and cry, though not the tears that swirled and tickled
as we unloaded my bags
and ran to the gate or even the tears
that shimmered my eyesight, turning hugs
into seizures,
waves into paralysis,
but something newer: contortions that bruised, tears serrated,
        squeezing
screaming
        acidic
leaking

                    clawing their way
                              across my face
like angry piranhas
                              at war
on the surface.
Thankful,
at least, for not being noticed by the man on my right who
lifts, unfolds
and crinkles his newspaper,
or the man on my left who adjusts his headphones,
his wife who is reading her book,
these stewardesses telling us all what to do
in case of emergency.

I am too busy with memory. My
favorite:

Buried deep on your couch
in blankets and cushions, we're smoking a joint
and listening to Sarah sing quietly
of "Elsewhere."
We giggle and glide, we writhe even higher
and stare, caress,
decoding our secrets. I am
bubbles all over.
Is it love that bulges like a well-fed embryo inside of my heart,
elbowing its walls, that kicks and stretches?

I will never forget,
as the plane speeds up and rises for takeoff, the weight of
your lips,
your tongue with its metal piercing
moving across,
                              down

around
inside of my mouth,
or your hands that, even now
still echo
        here
underneath my clothing.

FOR SHAWN

1. Shawn, with a book of poems

Not begun, but it will begin
like anything
meant never to happen—kismet caught up to
by one of its targets,
the tumbleweed heart rolling
easily across a
man
    to
        man wasteland, a bookstore open until 11 pm.

A cursory glance:
your long-fingered hand seen
curving around,
involving that book of poetry by Paul Monette, tucked away
and cross-legged,
book
    open,
propped casually upon your
denim-clad knee,
fluctuating change of expressions, foot tap-tap-tapping,
the handsomest face
honing in
on meaning, another long-fingered hand
against your temple.

"Good book,"
then I'm around the corner, behind the bookshelves, a hit
and run glimpse, at
once

a beginning point for the imagination, my hook
awaiting
a curious nibble.

    2. in echo

To think of you now, as then,
beneath
that liquid knitting of dreamlike music: jazz
with piano,
harmonized humming in saxophone whirlpools,
a candlelit bedroom. Your
flesh like icing on a moon-white
newborn,

hair that my tongue swam slowly through from
nipple to nipple, from chest to
waistline,
down below the belt: the sweat sweetened core of longed for
precedence,
your long-lost erection, when sighing, I
can taste.

    3. for a fuck

Who could blame, even you, for
a fuck
like that, for coercing me over and onto all fours,
both knees apart,
hands helping to simulate a broken
                                    neck

with my head pressed harder at an angle acute and quite
unnatural
to the rest of my body,

my sandpapered cheek, my ear, my
mouth
in a friction against the

        cold
navy blue
of the headboard wall.
Piled-up pillows and sheets like quiet, blind witnesses
at an electric
              execution who do
not look away, do not
unfurl
or cough dissent, but who endure the

        tremors.

The Last Time I Loved Him

Then, no. It is not
what I do not understand, a blur
of believing
here within my own nudity or even a hope that grows
like hair on the body, a fever
caught
       flying up close
from around your scrotum and against
my jaw line,
a tickle of hands unafraid, an external thing, every
word wiped clean.
No. It was not even that. But, still,

I moved to this city where your left hand had pulled me
and I lay in my bed on the familiar
stains
in a strange new bedroom
and there it was.
It waited, it slithered deliberate like trembling hands
inside of my bloodstream,
a thickness crawling with tarantula legs
along nerves and
muscle,
it aroused itself, became swollen, engorged
behind the eye of my nipple
and dreamed
that your right-handed finger might burrow erect
and discover its center. It
exists
like breath. It is sweeter than absence.

For two months it mattered, molding candle wax flesh
collected in puddles,
bending the flames of our branches
in toward the coldness.
How the visits dwindled and more than ever I would lick your sweat
from beneath my fingernails,
see your name unwind like a whisper
and shimmer
across the lips of strangers, even bite the goodbye
off of every kiss
my reflection gave me in the darkened
train window.
It grumbled like hunger, at last,
amazed.
It twirled like winds among the will and subconscious.
It outgrew its depth, ignoring
each clap of thunder the mind portended while dipping its feet
in a poolside oasis
the libido had made. I could only agree

it was the distance that hurt us,
your answers
themselves, only ends of the rope, a distorted parade
of equivocations you phrased politely
and led in a tour
                    around
     the table
at lunch,
         the last time I saw you. My face,
my hands, every curve into privacy
bubbled with grief,

my clothing upon me like ants
awakening
and I carried it hidden.

It was there in my pocket, climbing downward and deeper
on throughout my stomach, squirmed
like sweat-filled
worms
underneath my arms and at the back of my neck,
even listening in. It admitted its pain,
as soft as instinct. It
blinded itself
and yet it would witness. It knew what it was. It is all

or nothing. It survives like death,
unraveling hate.
It is hotter than lava before it has cooled and
hardened.

COLD

They say that I am cold,
immune
        and numb,
withdrawn to a far-off horizon on a tundra of words
and blinking, yet
blind
underneath the snowfall. Even so,

I have dreamt of you
like lava
hot chocolate inside of my igloo-
hard
hermetic heart,
crouched over myself
and threading it through—a needle, my skin, this sewing
a fire
into layers of breathing. As I have imagined—

a scent of sweat,
every hair in a suddenly shivering wave
rising up against your shadow's approach, all liquid black
condensed
into parting lips that douse my neck,
your fingertips
sliding
like four
        long
                streams
pulled
        down
by gravity across my stomach, then

below the waistline.
Warmer
with dusk, burning slow at the edges, I am patient, deceived
and hiding
alone—my love
a coal
and two hands groping
the bare
    ice
      walls.

HOT ASS

It's a finger, at first, that
                        slides
into pleasure in search of the sweating
slow breath of taboo, an
abstract core.
A swelling of smell
among imminent moves.
It's a hot ass burning like a long afternoon. You pose,
perspiring. Your tongue
rubs sparks
against warm fallen timbers, reluctant, then wet
like a downward pivot. A day
where rain
hits
     staccato like bullets
against window blockades, shadows drip from the ceiling.
Rivers rekindle. The fabric
absorbs.

Only one "hello" and I had shed my clothes, unraveling
nude
in a fold-out bed as your hands turned over
the coals of my skin. You pause,
peripheral.
Coming in closer, a red
below
     you heating in swirls and eating the walls
out of all their whiteness.
In yellows and orange we meet
at last—
a smoldering throat, your casual match,
entwining within. A
kiss
that implodes.

Names, Like Fingers

I have them here. They roll in waves
and wave to me
"goodbye,"
           "hello." They come and go. Slip by, a breeze
into forms unfolding and eddying faces that
rivet
the eyes like sounds I can see
swimming deep within. They touch my arms
and grip
like perforations, purple-hued kisses
with a black-yellow edge.

They float
           over pavement. Again, I feel their
honey slide down
in around each hair along my body. It
shreds the spine into white
spaghetti,
the brain dissolves its weight in bubbles. A tongue
now bleeds and
pushes inference beyond its tip. I've

no words left, no pride to speak
or call you back, to
ask
or plead. I lick every name like an index finger, turn
then toss each page,
           hit
and missed
in the jostle of loving these boys
who could've been language

as silence congeals,
shut
between my lips that stick together.

Here

Again, I hide
where afternoons linger, drift longer and lazy, outstretched, uncurled,
getting warmer despite this February wind,
your words turning wet
in the heat of the fire. I'm here.
You're gone.

If you do return after these weeks of silence, lift up
my curtains and
break
my windows, you'll witness the anguish
of a quivering body
left alone again to rise
and fall
by its own right hand. If so, turn off the lights. Swim into
my bedroom. Uncover me
writhing with all I have circumvented—eventual love,
having seen it before
like a tornado of anguish, even said it like
shrapnel
sliding off of the tongue. If so, then

come,
lie down like a liar, undress
the deceived.
Perspire, revere,
begin to explore where you once adventured, push
harder and
savor
my resistance igniting,

put it back in perspective, awaiting the frenzy like a heathen
aroused, a believer
in magic.
Our verge is lit. Lean over.
Dive in.

Sunday night out in the East Village

There was nothing there but flesh
on fire,
swimming limbs in a sea of men. I waded in
against the current,
through arms like waves that crashed in silence, rolling in
and easing out
across
and slipping beneath my surface
over and under.

A pirouette
among cocks and lava
fueling each sudden impulsive fellatio, that hairline trail
toward Mt. Vesuvius. And I was there,
like them,
erect, about to erupt
and scald the mouth of this man who has come here
to engulf the
flames.
        To smell,

then feel it,
this snail-crawling sweat down the curves of our backs, our
moistening hair
in dank matted armpits, slithering
along
like elongating tongues. We were breathing humidity,
this steam we created. Hotter
and damp
we looked around us and it fogged our vision.
We hushed our conscience, then

led the way
and like the blind we used
our hands to see.

FOR STEVE

1. Right Now

8 p.m.
and we've left our meeting—you went
your way
and now I am here among all these strangers
on a train going home;
with every roar that rattles and
shakes my reverie back
and forth
I feel it still—your hand
sliding over my knee, the embrace goodbye, that
pliable warmth
as we pressed together, a kiss only
imagined.

2. In Bed, At Last

Even now, I'm unsure how you created this fire
you've set—a light in my armor of winter;
where ice endured, you have sparked desire
and shattered the cold in a flurry of splinters.
With every breath, you fog my surface,
melt the edges and burn these blues
into reds and yellows, a quick sudden bliss
of expanding orange. You lit the fuse
and conquered the darkness. I'd waited forever
for hands to warm my frozen body,
lips like yours to rub together
with mine—ignite. It is you who've thawed me,
made numbing snow into puddles of feeling,
brought summer in as December was leaving.

3. *Hands*

Home by four
in the afternoon, caressing my keys that are warm
yet cold,
I let myself in
and lock us in. I stand, then

move, the windows
and blinds
my hands bring down. My apartment darkens.
I am here alone.
I walk the path you walked
before
from room to room, from
table to chair,
from couch to bed. I am afraid to sit
and lose my way
as smiles and love tumble out from pockets of memory like
crumbs to mark
each well-worn step, where tears still slide
and drip
in floods to wash
you and all that you touched
downstream into nothing.

Every thought of us is a threadbare burn
in my chest and
head.
I feel my hands that wring
in twists and
turn together having lost their purpose. Still,
they know
what they once were for: your hand
to hold, your skin to savor

like dampened silk,
your red-bearded cheek to stroke as though my fingers were
kissing you
over and over, your unclothed body
to outline slowly,
your heart
to feel in throbs of love. But now,

there's nothing.

4. Come

      Slow,
yet sudden, you
come
to mind as I lock my door and run toward distraction,
a train escape,
Manhattan diversions. But
there you are in every doorway, in
every boy
whose eyes undress my perspiring body and
glance away,
in a soundtrack followed from store to store. You moan my name
at every corner,
caress
      my shoulder
in crowds that swarm and ebb and flow in sun and
shadow.

You come—a drop
into rippling memory, a torrid heart. You
drip
like this and then
diffuse,
easing along each highway vein and slackened muscle, you

find your way
in behind the barricade, melt the ice of hate and anger.
You push.
        You pull.
You're passing throughout me and
lightning slithers
in paths you make, it drags behind, it marks
your tread.
        It's then I know,

you've come again
and taken hold, surrounding my heart like tongues of lava to
lick
my wounds. I breathe cologne. I
stop,
        then go.
There is only home, to unlock the door and cry alone.
I shut the blinds and evening falls.
The bed is cold,
though my skin is warm and these hands like yours
explore up close,
remembering
how your touch evolved and led me on, both
finger
        and palm,
how your kisses fell like boiling water in-between the handprints.
It reminds me now of how it felt
to rise
        and twist
and burn
up whole against your body. I bite my lip and sigh,
explode.

5. shattered, broken

You and I sit
in the Factory Café where we've come to talk, but
words are daggers,
language is bleach that burns away meaning;
by your decision—"us"

dissolved.

"My life," you say, "isn't less without you. We're
two different people."
I turn my face. "You don't engage,
you're not outgoing." The dam has broken. I'm buried alive
and begin to dig
down past your countenance, remind you how
we entwined our bodies, a give
and take
in all our kisses, the way you loved to feel me naked.
You only say, "I still want to jump you, here,
right now,"

when you no longer love me. I'm lost,
confused.
I fall against the walls around you as floors cave in and
lamps unravel.
Your goodbye fence
has cold, sharp edges, hard and gray, that
crack my eyes
like eggs of sadness the more I run and crash upon it,
my heart in shreds
embedded
deep inside my breathing. Inhaling slow, I stand, then sway,
with punctured dreams and leaking bliss.
I cannot think. I walk away

and leave you sitting, freezing warm and watching intently,
these remnants
in motion.

I am out of the door and maneuvering home, but now
only half of what, with you,
I always
believed I was.

6. Quilts and Blankets

Quilts and blankets
come,
hide this heart far beneath your waves
of soothing cotton,
                    flow
up across my legs, my torso, my arms, submerge this sadness.
Build a lid
over tears and touching, my hands that
grope
and can't forget his body that rumbled against my own
here within your depths.
I am now alone.

                    Please,
clump and mold
into longer soft edges, then seep in slowly to fill up his absence,
keep me warm,
though discontented. Envelop the hurt.
Settle in place
and surround my breathing,
let me expand and reach your surface, grip and tug and
pull you closer
finger
        by finger to cling

in tight like desire-
proof clothing, a thicker skin that withstands all feeling. Hover above,
then slide like dusk toward the bed's horizon,
darken this error,
                      thunder
then pour
and flood this desert I'm lying upon,
bury his scent like a long-lost treasure along the bottom.
Cover me whole,
prevent the day from exposing a love he ripped
and shredded
before he went home.

7. Frustration

Why can't I turn and shake you loose
like a coat in summer and leave you lying
behind, discarded here upon the carpet?
I can't get free, yet I keep on trying,

run and jump and twist and tumble,
tug these sleeves of you I'm wearing.
I cry and I pull at every button
but it's only me I end up tearing.

8. 3:56 a.m.

I could not fall asleep because of the pain,
a head that hurt, a heart still broken;
yet, even now I cannot explain,
for what I write should not be spoken—
my thoughts of you, this strange desire,
all resentment devoured by hungry fears.
I tried to cry and put out the fire,

but poetry came instead of tears,
so I held myself with my own two hands
and made-believe in your love again,
selecting, then swallowing various brands
of where to go and where I have been;
all night in my bed and still wide awake,
every jerk of the pen, with a dull, steady ache.

    9. If I were asked

I'd confess, I'm holding my love not by its handle
but its blade,
like scissors I'm running with
double-edged hope
into slip and slide scenes
of us
together. At 12:00,
an alchemy of hate into you at last. I dive
without air, past
the abyss of
        "maybe."

You just didn't know. My heart
was always there,
though hidden beneath my see-through surface, behind
my eyes
that looked for you in every crowd,
sought you out
above all others and always under a firework sky
of smiles and laughter
that rose
and burst and fell
into nothing.

10. with you

I wake sometimes
and the room is warm.

I lick my lips and my legs uncurl
as one by one each
fingertip glides
across my flesh in long thin lines of perspiration.
Ah, yes,

      I know
how even in sleep and here alone,
I have been with you.
I've tossed and turned, stirred up your sweat
from the sheets and pillows,
untied the depths
and then dived below.

11. Again

Once again, you came from nowhere,
disengaged
your scent, your self
from the backdrop monotony, suddenly separate
like oil from water,
you flowed
then settled in face to face while everyone else
swam in circles around us. These
men behind me,
on my left and right, at every angle. Yet, I was dancing alone
with Joe and Edgar.

And then you found it, hidden in jealousy—your love
for me
you had said was gone. It roared,
it awakened
as you crossed the room,
your hand up against my shoulder like a match striking flint,
your arms
constricting, holding me in,

your grinning quick
kisses
and abrasive beard friction, the kneading
of chests
and our stomachs together, of anxious fingers in a
rediscovery of favorite secrets in winks
and glances,
in public euphoria.

How Obvious, Then

At 5 a.m., awake and blinking, third day in a row
with a terrible headache,
I am here
in the dark of our dark blue bedroom, our
curtains shut
where morning is evening. From within your arms and
beneath the blanket
I emerge and
stumble
and bump my knee, step around the bed and out of the door
in search of an aspirin.
It's as I'm returning that you lift your head to ask,
still half in your dream, "You okay?
What's wrong?" Like couples elsewhere,
we've learned
to speak in our own vernacular, to know that this
from you
means how much you love me.

                                        How you say "my boyfriend..."
when teasing my actions or
explaining my habits, a reference to me as
something of yours,
a favorite thing kept warm in your pocket, familiar
and close; in these boxers
you bought
and then at home requested, "Try them on," watching me move
in smiles and longing. It's a kiss
on my shoulder
when you're half-asleep,
the doors

you open and even my hand you caress indirectly.

I come back to bed, slip in
to entangle
against your body and answer, "I have a headache. I took some aspirin."
Like couples elsewhere,
we all have had the same conversation. You know that this
from me,
in a disguise of diction, means
"I love you too"—
                        a reworded truth
in these early morning hours.

Acknowledgments

Grateful acknowledgement is given to *Assaracus*, *Down in the Dirt*, *Gay City*, *The Gay & Lesbian Review Worldwide*, and *Ganymede*, where some of these poems first appeared.

About the Poet

A native Floridian, Christopher Gaskins moved to New York City in 1999 looking for the hustle and bustle he'd always heard so much about, but eventually he came to his senses and returned home in the summer of 2012. He currently lives in Orlando, where he teaches high school English. His poems have appeared in such journals as *The Gay & Lesbian Review Worldwide*, *Ganymede*, *Open Minds Quarterly*, *Darkling*, *Pearl*, *Chroma* and in the anthologies *Sanctified* and *Gay City*.

About the Publisher

Founded in 2010, Sibling Rivalry Press is an independent publishing house based in Alexander, Arkansas. Our mission is to publish work that disturbs and enraptures. We are proud to be the home to *Assaracus*, the world's only print journal of gay male poetry. Our titles have been honored by the American Library Association through inclusion on its annual "Over the Rainbow" list of recommended LGBT reading and by *Library Journal*, who named *Assaracus* as a best new magazine of 2011. While we champion our LGBTIQ authors and artists, we are an inclusive publishing house and welcome all authors, artists, and readers regardless of sexual orientation or identity.

www.siblingrivalrypress.com

www.ingramcontent.com/pod-product-compliance
Lightning Source LLC
LaVergne TN
LVHW041339080426
835512LV00006B/528